THE OFFICIAL DICTIONARY OF SARCASM POSTCARDS

W9-AGA-268

45 Cards for Those of Us
Who Are Better and Smarter
Than the Rest of You

JAMES NAPOLI

STERLING
New York

STERLING
New York

An Imprint of Sterling Publishing
387 Park Avenue South
New York, NY 10016

STERLING and the distinctive Sterling logo are registered trademarks of Sterling Publishing Co., Inc.

Published in 2014 by Sterling Publishing Co., Inc.

Adapted from *The Official Dictionary of Sarcasm*, © 2010 by Sterling Publishing Co., Inc.

All rights reserved. No part of this publication may be reproduced, stored in a retrieval system, or transmitted in any form or by any means (including electronic, mechanical, photocopying, recording, or otherwise) without prior written permission from the publisher.

ISBN 978-1-4549-1391-7

Distributed in Canada by Sterling Publishing
℅ Canadian Manda Group, 165 Dufferin Street
Toronto, Ontario, Canada M6K 3H6
Distributed in the United Kingdom by GMC Distribution Services
Castle Place, 166 High Street, Lewes, East Sussex, England BN7 1XU
Distributed in Australia by Capricorn Link (Australia) Pty. Ltd.
P.O. Box 704, Windsor, NSW 2756, Australia

For information about custom editions, special sales, and premium and corporate purchases,
please contact Sterling Special Sales at 800-805-5489 or specialsales@sterlingpublishing.com.

All illustrations by Andy Taray and Christy Taray for Ohioboy Art & Design / www.ohioboy.com

Manufactured in China

2 4 6 8 10 9 7 5 3 1

www.sterlingpublishing.com

INTRODUCTION

Though it hardly matters to a sarcastic person (who is most assuredly not in the business of making anyone feel better), those who appreciate sarcasm are a rare breed. Two major forces are at work: the desire to provoke and the desire to seek the truth. Both of these life missions can make people very uncomfortable. You now hold in your hands the perfect form for spreading the word of sarcasm, eviscerating the innards of propriety, and puncturing the balloon of pretension.

Use these postcards to challenge the tiny minds of the plebeian rabble with whom you're forced to communicate. You've been waiting patiently for a way to impart your wisdom upon the uninspired masses. And now here it is. Not that you give a crap.

+

BARISTA:

A PERSON HIGHLY SKILLED IN WRITING YOUR FIRST NAME IN SHARPIE ON THE SIDE OF A HEAT-TREATED PAPER CUP.

© 2014 by Sterling Publishing Co., Inc.

THE OFFICIAL
DICTIONARY of
SARCASM

ART STUDENT:

THE SIGNIFICANT OTHER WHO MAKES LIVING ON CAT FOOD FEEL LIKE A BOLD DECLARATION OF YOUR LOVE.

Kittay

FOR KITIES
&
ART STUDENTS

© 2014 by Sterling Publishing Co., Inc.

THE **OFFICIAL**
DICTIONARY OF
SARCASM

ANIMALS:

CREATURES THAT LEAVE US VERY FEW
OPTIONS BESIDES HUNTING THEM,
EATING THEM, KEEPING THEM AS PETS,
OR LOCKING THEM IN A CAGE. THAT'S
JUST HOW IT IS WHEN YOU HOLD
DOMINION OVER ALL NATURE.

© 2014 by Sterling Publishing Co., Inc.

THE **OFFICIAL**
DICTIONARY OF
SARCASM

BEATLES, THE:

OBSCURE LIVERPOOL ROCK AND ROLL BAND OF VERY LITTLE NOTE OR INFLUENCE.

© 2014 by Sterling Publishing Co., Inc.

THE OFFICIAL DICTIONARY OF SARCASM

BICYCLE:

A PEDAL-DRIVEN, HUMAN-POWERED
CONVEYANCE USED BY PEOPLE
WHO THINK THEY'RE MAKING SOME
KIND OF BIG STATEMENT ABOUT THE
ENVIRONMENT JUST BY RIDING ONE.

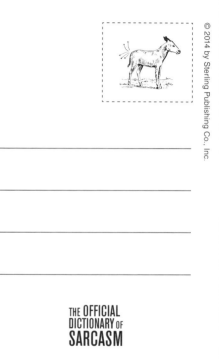

© 2014 by Sterling Publishing Co., Inc.

THE OFFICIAL DICTIONARY OF SARCASM

BIG BEN:

A BIG CLOCK. ONLY THE
BRITISH WOULD THINK
THAT WAS ANYTHING.

© 2014 by Sterling Publishing Co., Inc.

THE **OFFICIAL**
DICTIONARY OF
SARCASM

COMMITMENT:

1. THE ACT OF BINDING ONESELF TO A SPECIFIC PATH—USUALLY AS REGARDS A RELATIONSHIP WITH A ROMANTIC PARTNER.
2. CONSIGNMENT TO A MENTAL HEALTH FACILITY.
3. THERE MAY BE NO DIFFERENCE BETWEEN 1 AND 2.

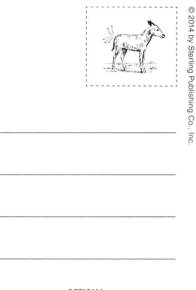

© 2014 by Sterling Publishing Co., Inc.

THE **OFFICIAL**
DICTIONARY OF
SARCASM

COMMON COLD, THE:

SOMETHING GOD INFLICTS UPON HUMANS EVERY SO OFTEN TO GENTLY REMIND US THAT WE ARE 90 PERCENT SNOT.

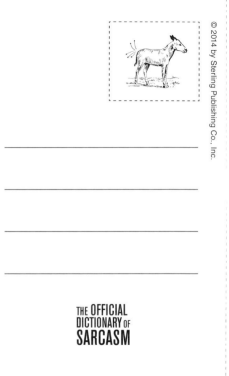

© 2014 by Sterling Publishing Co., Inc.

THE OFFICIAL
DICTIONARY OF
SARCASM

COMPATIBLE:

THE STATE OF BEING ABLE TO COEXIST
CONGENIALLY. FOR HUMAN BEINGS, IT IS
FAR MORE ACHIEVABLE WITH DOGS.

© 2014 by Sterling Publishing Co., Inc.

THE **OFFICIAL**
DICTIONARY OF
SARCASM

DISCOVERY
CHANNEL:

SHARKS.

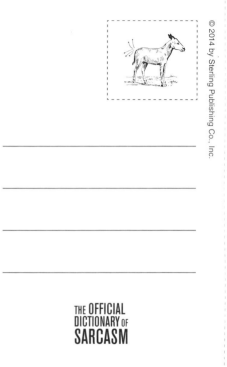

© 2014 by Sterling Publishing Co., Inc.

THE **OFFICIAL**
DICTIONARY OF
SARCASM

DRINKING:

A LEISURE ACTIVITY THAT ALLOWS YOU TO RATIONALIZE YOUR NEED TO BLOT OUT THE HIDEOUS REALITIES OF YOUR LIFE BY CONVINCING YOU THAT IF YOU DO ENOUGH OF IT YOU WILL MEET THE PERSON WHO WILL BLOT THEM OUT INSTEAD.

© 2014 by Sterling Publishing Co., Inc.

THE **OFFICIAL**
DICTIONARY OF
SARCASM

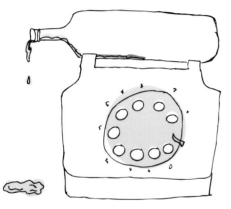

DRUNK DIALING:

THE VAIN HOPE THAT SLURRING YOUR WORDS OVER A CELL PHONE AT THREE-THIRTY IN THE MORNING WILL CONVINCE THE PERSON WHO DUMPED YOU SIX YEARS AGO TO SUDDENLY WANT YOU WAY BAD.

© 2014 by Sterling Publishing Co., Inc.

THE OFFICIAL DICTIONARY OF SARCASM

FACEBOOK:

A HANDY WAY TO INVITE POTENTIAL STALKERS TO BROWSE THROUGH HUNDREDS OF PHOTOGRAPHS OF YOU, YOUR FAMILY, AND FRIENDS.

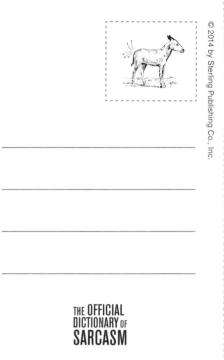

© 2014 by Sterling Publishing Co., Inc.

THE **OFFICIAL**
DICTIONARY OF
SARCASM

FIGHT:

THE UNFORTUNATE, BUT SADLY UNAVOIDABLE, SIDE EFFECT OF
KNOWING THAT YOUR IDIOT PARTNER IS THE ONE WHO'S WRONG.

© 2014 by Sterling Publishing Co., Inc.

THE **OFFICIAL**
DICTIONARY OF
SARCASM

FLOWERS:

COLORFUL, FRAGRANT
APOLOGIES.

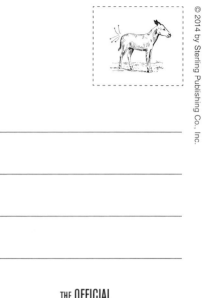

© 2014 by Sterling Publishing Co., Inc.

THE **OFFICIAL**
DICTIONARY OF
SARCASM

FOOTBALL:
AVOIDANCE OF INTIMACY,
WITH SEXIST COMMERCIALS.

© 2014 by Sterling Publishing Co., Inc.

THE **OFFICIAL**
DICTIONARY OF
SARCASM

GASOLINE:
AN UNREGULATED FORM OF CRACK
USED WITH IMPUNITY BY EVERYONE
IN THE FREE WORLD.

© 2014 by Sterling Publishing Co., Inc.

THE **OFFICIAL**
DICTIONARY OF
SARCASM

GEEK:

SOMEONE WITH AN ECCENTRIC DEVOTION TO SOME ASPECT OF POPULAR CULTURE, SUCH AS *STAR WARS* OR VIDEO GAMING. WHILE IN THE NOT-TOO-DISTANT PAST THIS TYPE OF ANTISOCIAL LOSER WOULD HAVE BEEN RELEGATED TO HIS BEDROOM, THANKS TO THE INTERNET HE IS NOW DEEMED SORT OF HOT, AND EVEN HAS A FAIR-TO-MIDDLING CHANCE OF GETTING SOME ACTION.

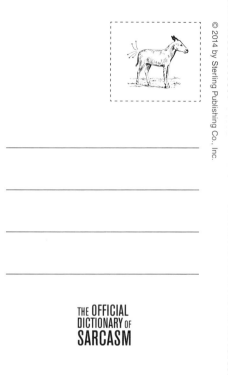

© 2014 by Sterling Publishing Co., Inc.

THE **OFFICIAL** **DICTIONARY** OF **SARCASM**

GOLDFISH:

A CREATURE SPECIALLY BRED TO PROVIDE YOUNG CHILDREN EARLY TRAINING IN FLUSHING SOMETHING DEAD DOWN THE TOILET.

© 2014 by Sterling Publishing Co., Inc.

THE **OFFICIAL**
DICTIONARY OF
SARCASM

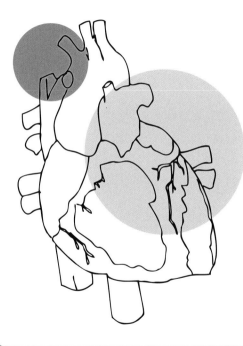

HEART:

THE CHAMBERED ORGAN THAT
PUMPS BLOOD THROUGH THE
CIRCULATORY SYSTEM. OFTEN SAID
TO BE THE LOCUS OF HUMAN LOVE
AND DEEPER FEELING. WHICH
MIGHT EXPLAIN WHY IT LOOKS LIKE
A WEEK-OLD CUT OF RANCID STEAK.

© 2014 by Sterling Publishing Co., Inc.

THE **OFFICIAL**
DICTIONARY OF
SARCASM

ICE CREAM:

THE DAIRY INDUSTRY'S GIFT TO THOSE
WHO HAVE JUST BEEN DUMPED.

© 2014 by Sterling Publishing Co., Inc.

THE OFFICIAL
DICTIONARY OF
SARCASM

INDEPENDENT:

FULLY CAPABLE OF BEING OUT OF A
RELATIONSHIP FOR SEVERAL MONTHS AND
NOT RESORTING TO INTOXICANTS, CURLING UP
IN A FETAL POSITION, OR HOOKING UP ONLINE.

© 2014 by Sterling Publishing Co., Inc.

THE **OFFICIAL**
DICTIONARY OF
SARCASM

IPHONE:

A DEVICE THAT ALLOWS NERDS TO CONSTANTLY TOUCH SOMETHING BESIDES THEMSELVES.

© 2014 by Sterling Publishing Co., Inc.

THE OFFICIAL
DICTIONARY OF
SARCASM

KITTEN:
GOD'S WAY OF LETTING MEN KNOW
HOW UNIMPORTANT THEY ARE.

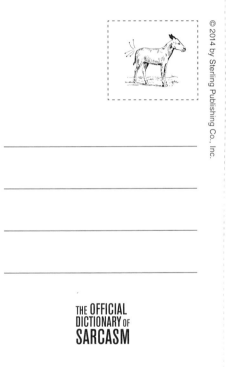

© 2014 by Sterling Publishing Co., Inc.

THE **OFFICIAL**
DICTIONARY OF
SARCASM

MEDIA:
LIARS WITH ACCESS TO EYE-CATCHING GRAPHICS.

© 2014 by Sterling Publishing Co., Inc.

THE **OFFICIAL**
DICTIONARY OF
SARCASM

MOTHER:

1. THE WOMAN WHO ENDURED MANY HOURS OF EXCRUCIATING PAIN TO BRING YOU INTO THE WORLD AND WHOM YOU REPAY FOR THIS SACRIFICE BY STAYING SINGLE AND DRIFTING FROM JOB TO JOB, NOT EVEN CARING THAT WITH EACH FOOLISH MISSTEP YOU MAKE, YOU DRIVE A HOT SABER DEEPER AND DEEPER INTO HER HEART. AND DON'T EVER FORGET THAT SHE LOVES YOU.
2. A SAINT. (ITALIAN AMERICAN MEN ONLY.)

© 2014 by Sterling Publishing Co., Inc.

THE **OFFICIAL**
DICTIONARY OF
SARCASM

MOUSTACHE:

A TYPE OF FACIAL HAIR THAT LETS THE WORLD KNOW YOU HAVE NOT FORGOTTEN THE 1970S, BAD PORN, OR TOM SELLECK.

© 2014 by Sterling Publishing Co., Inc.

THE **OFFICIAL**
DICTIONARY OF
SARCASM

NEWS:

WAR, MURDER, NATURAL
DISASTERS, AND A FAILING
ECONOMY SERVED IN CONVENIENT,
EASY-TO-FORGET TWO-MINUTE
INCREMENTS AND TOPPED OFF
WITH AN INSPIRING STORY OF
COURAGE ABOUT EITHER AN
ORANGUTAN OR SOMEBODY
WITH A TUMOR

© 2014 by Sterling Publishing Co., Inc.

THE **OFFICIAL**
DICTIONARY OF
SARCASM

OFFICE:

1. THE PLACE WHERE ALL THE SOUL-SUCKING FAERIES LIVE.
2. THE LAST LOCATION ON EARTH WHERE THERE IS ALWAYS AT LEAST ONE PERSON WHO IS STILL INTO GARFIELD.

© 2014 by Sterling Publishing Co., Inc.

THE **OFFICIAL**
DICTIONARY OF
SARCASM

PET:

A CREATURE THAT UPLIFTS YOU
WITH ITS CONSISTENT SHOWING OF
PURE, UNCONDITIONAL LOVE. THE
FACT THAT IT CAN DO THIS BECAUSE
IT HAS NEITHER THE POWER OF
SPEECH NOR IS CAPABLE OF
GRASPING THE IRRITATING EXTENT
OF YOUR NEUROTIC HABITS REMAINS
CONVENIENTLY BESIDE THE POINT.

© 2014 by Sterling Publishing Co., Inc.

THE **OFFICIAL**
DICTIONARY OF
SARCASM

PREGNANT:
FAT WITH A SENSE OF PURPOSE.

© 2014 by Sterling Publishing Co., Inc.

THE **OFFICIAL**
DICTIONARY OF
SARCASM

QUEEN:

SLANG FOR HOMOSEXUAL,
MUCH TO THE CHAGRIN OF
BRITISH ROYALTY.

© 2014 by Sterling Publishing Co., Inc.

THE **OFFICIAL**
DICTIONARY OF
SARCASM

QUIRK:

AN UNUSUAL, UNCOMMON
PERSONALITY TRAIT. SUCH AS BEING
CONSIDERATE, OR RETURNING CALLS
WITHIN TWENTY-FOUR HOURS.

© 2014 by Sterling Publishing Co., Inc.

THE **OFFICIAL**
DICTIONARY OF
SARCASM

RHYTHM:

SOMETHING POSSESSED BY A TOTAL
OF SEVEN WHITE PEOPLE.

© 2014 by Sterling Publishing Co., Inc.

THE **OFFICIAL**
DICTIONARY OF
SARCASM

ROCK STAR:

WHAT HAPPENS WHEN THE ID IS
GIVEN A DECENT SINGING VOICE.

© 2014 by Sterling Publishing Co., Inc.

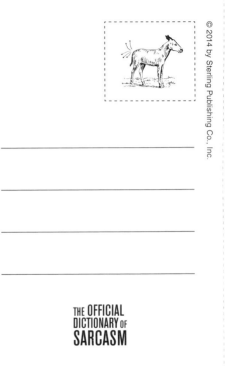

THE **OFFICIAL**
DICTIONARY OF
SARCASM

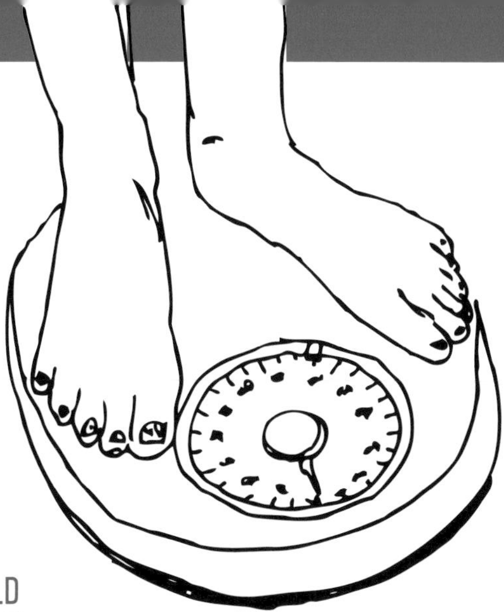

SCALE:

THE ONE THING IN THE WORLD THAT NEVER RELINQUISHES ITS SUPERIORITY OVER YOU, NO MATTER HOW MANY TIMES YOU LOOK DOWN ON IT.

© 2014 by Sterling Publishing Co., Inc.

THE **OFFICIAL**
DICTIONARY OF
SARCASM

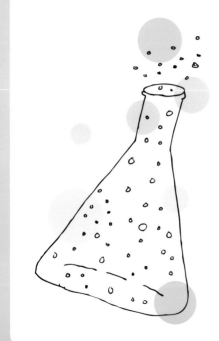

SCIENTIST:

A PERSON IN A LAB COAT WHO APPEARS AT THE BEGINNING OF SCIENCE FICTION FILMS TO EXPLAIN HOW THE COLLISION OF CERTAIN ISOTOPES CAN RESULT IN A HALF-MAN-HALF-LEMUR.

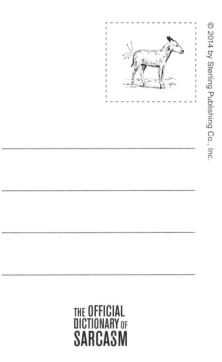

© 2014 by Sterling Publishing Co., Inc.

THE OFFICIAL
DICTIONARY OF
SARCASM

SKIING:

POPULAR WINTERTIME ACTIVITY AND
OPPORTUNITY TO MEET OTHER LUNATICS
WHO SHARE YOUR INTEREST NOT ONLY
IN CAREENING INTO TREES BUT ALSO IN
GETTING FROSTBITE WHILE DOING IT.

© 2014 by Sterling Publishing Co., Inc.

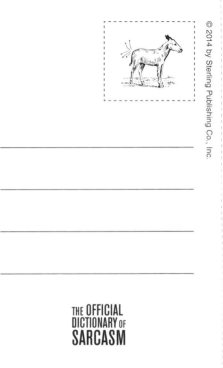

THE **OFFICIAL**
DICTIONARY OF
SARCASM

SKYDIVING:
PLUNGING TO ONE'S DEATH,
INTERRUPTED.

© 2014 by Sterling Publishing Co., Inc.

THE **OFFICIAL**
DICTIONARY OF
SARCASM

SOCIAL NETWORKING:

A WAY OF IMAGINING THAT YOU STILL HAVE SOCIAL SKILLS AND CAN NETWORK EVEN THOUGH YOU ARE SURGICALLY ATTACHED TO YOUR COMPUTER AND NEVER LEAVE YOUR HOUSE.

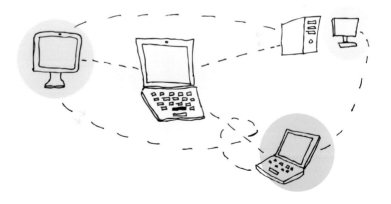

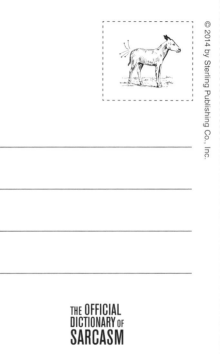

© 2014 by Sterling Publishing Co., Inc.

THE **OFFICIAL**
DICTIONARY OF
SARCASM

THERAPIST:

SOMEONE WHO POINTS OUT THE UNCONSCIOUS AND UNHEALTHY RELATIONSHIP PATTERNS IN YOUR LIFE THAT YOU FORGET ABOUT BETWEEN SESSIONS AS YOU RUIN MORE LIVES, INCLUDING YOUR OWN.

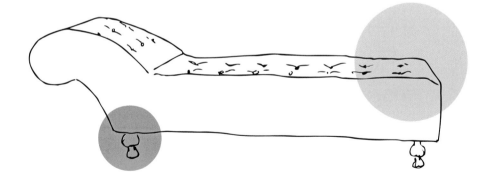

© 2014 by Sterling Publishing Co., Inc.

THE OFFICIAL
DICTIONARY OF
SARCASM

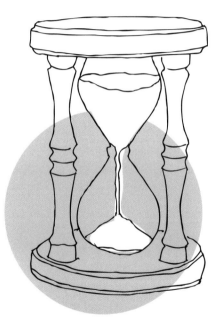

TIME:

AN ABSTRACT CONCEPT THAT CAUGHT ON ABOUT SIX THOUSAND YEARS AGO AND RESULTED IN THE CONCEPTS OF BOTH THE DEADLINE AND THE HEART ATTACK, IN THAT ORDER.

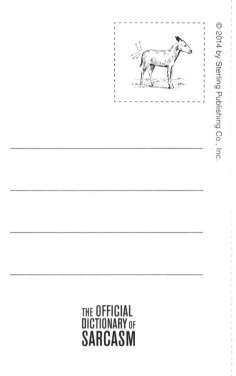

© 2014 by Sterling Publishing Co., Inc.

THE **OFFICIAL**
DICTIONARY OF
SARCASM

VACATION:

WHAT YOU TAKE WITH YOUR SIGNIFICANT OTHER OR FAMILY, KNOWING FULL WELL THAT NOT BEING WITH ANY OF THEM WOULD BE THE REAL VACATION.

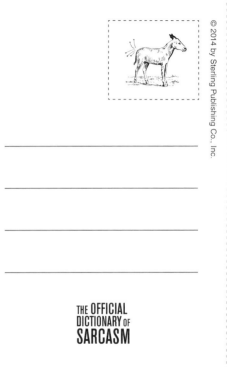

© 2014 by Sterling Publishing Co., Inc.

THE **OFFICIAL**
DICTIONARY OF
SARCASM

WINE:

A BEVERAGE THAT GIVES A TOUCH OF
CLASS TO THE PROCESS OF GETTING
SOMEONE DRUNK ENOUGH TO FIND
YOU ATTRACTIVE.

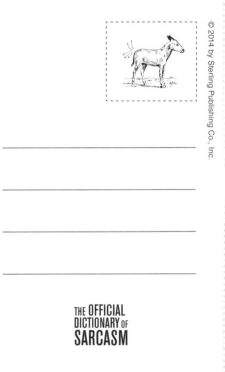

© 2014 by Sterling Publishing Co., Inc.

THE OFFICIAL
DICTIONARY OF
SARCASM

YOGA:

A SPIRITUAL DISCIPLINE AIMED AT GUIDING A PERSON TOWARD A DEEPER SENSE OF HIS OR HER OWN HUMANITY, WHOSE MOST WELL KNOWN POSITION IS THE DOWNWARD-FACING DOG.

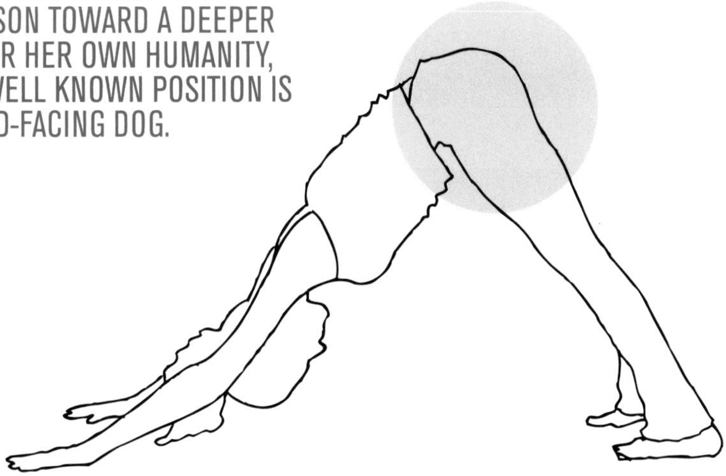

© 2014 by Sterling Publishing Co., Inc.

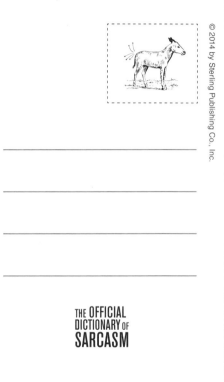

THE **OFFICIAL**
DICTIONARY OF
SARCASM

ABOUT THE AUTHOR

This is the part of the book where they tell you what other meaningless drivel the author has written, then it's on to whether the author is married and, if so, what the names of his or her spouse and children are. Oh, and then it's where the author lives, at which point it is always a good idea to imply that the author divides his or her time between two or more cities. It just seems much more writerly and gives one the impression that a reclusive, embittered fool is actually a cosmopolitan jet-setter.

Too bad you're not getting any of that.